雪謙文化

遇見·巴楚仁波切

（The Heart-Essence Advice on Two Ethics）

作者：巴楚仁波切（Patrul Rinpoche）

譯者：項慧齡

審定：劉婉俐

目錄

〔作者簡傳〕

巴楚仁波切簡傳

巴楚仁波切（Patrul Rinpoche，1808-1887）是一位得證的大師，雖然過著流浪漢般的生活，卻是上世紀最著名的精神導師之一。時至今日，人們對他的記憶仍非常鮮明，他是鼓舞藏傳佛教所有修行者的靈感泉源。

一八〇八年，巴楚仁波切出生於札秋喀（Dzachuka），地處雪謙（Shechen）和卓千（Dzogchen）北方的一處康藏遊牧區。幼年時的聰穎、善良和特殊能力，很快得到證實。他被認證為住在同一區的大師巴給・桑殿・彭措（Palge Samten Phuntshok）轉世，以曾建造一座刻有十萬塊六字大明咒[1]的石牆而聞名。後來，有幾位偉大上師認證他是寂天菩薩的化身，也有人認為他是吉美林巴尊者的語化身。這位年輕的巴給轉世——簡稱為「巴楚」，正式被推舉為其前世僧院的住持。

1　六字大明咒（Mani）：觀世音菩薩的心咒，共有六個字，唵嘛呢唄美吽（OM MANI PADME HUNG）。

　　不久之後，他遇到主要上師吉美・嘉威・紐古（Jigme Gyalwai Nyugu）。這位偉大的上師曾住在西藏中部多年，是吉美林巴最傑出的弟子之一，後來回到康區，獨自在接近雪線的粲瑪隆（Dzama Lung）僻遠山谷閉關數年。在他所住的迎風山坡上，甚至沒有山洞可以棲身，唯一的住所是地上的一個凹洞，靠著野菜、草根來維生。幾年過去後，這位非凡苦行者的聲名遠播。數以百計的弟子前來求見，在附近搭帳棚住了下來。吉美・嘉威・紐古是修行者的典範，生活極為儉樸，決心一直在那兒閉關直到徹底證悟。從吉美・嘉威・紐古處，巴楚仁波切接受了不下二十五次的《龍欽心髓》[2]前行[3]教授，以及其他許多重要法教。他非常精進地研習、修持這些法教。巴楚仁波切十幾歲時，曾花了很長一段時間在各地尋訪、隨侍上師——多數上師都居無定所。除了吉美・嘉威・紐古，巴楚仁波切還跟當時最重要的許多大師學習，包括第一世多竹千（the first Dodrup Chen）、吉美・欽列・偉瑟

2　《龍欽心髓》（Longchen Nyingthig）：或譯「龍欽寧體」，是關於寧瑪派最高修行心法大圓滿法的重要著作，由龍欽巴尊者所著，後來經過吉美林巴的整理，而成為寧瑪派必修的修行法要。

3　前行（Ngondro）：字義為「預備」、「基礎」、「先前」，能令修行增長的基礎修持。

（Jigme Trinle Oser）、吉美‧哦薩（Jigme Ngotsar）、多拉‧
吉美（Dola Jigme）、卓千寺的嘉瑟‧賢遍‧泰耶（Gyelse
Shenpen Thaye），以及大成就者多欽哲‧耶喜‧多傑（Do
Khyentse Yeshe Dorje）等。

　　多欽哲‧耶喜‧多傑是持明吉美林巴[4]的意化身，從小就
有天生的千里眼，示顯無數神通。巴楚仁波切對這位不尋常
的大師具有強烈的虔誠心，視其為佛。有一天，多欽哲在札
秋喀看到巴楚從附近經過時，大叫：「喂！巴給，過來！你不
敢嗎？」巴楚一走近，多欽哲便一把揪住他的頭髮，把他猛
摜在地上，然後在泥地上拖拉著。巴楚知道多欽哲醉得很厲
害，呼氣都透著酒味。他心想：「連這樣的大證悟者，也會醉
成這樣，做出不合理的舉動！」他的心裡浮現佛陀對飲酒過
失的闡釋。

　　就在這一刻，多欽哲突然鬆手放開巴楚，狠狠地瞪著他

4　吉美林巴（Jigme Lingpa，1729~1798）：著名的伏藏大師和大圓滿傳
　　承上師，龍欽巴尊者曾經化現在他面前三次，將完整的《龍欽心髓》
　　傳承給他，希望他保存並傳揚這些教法。吉美林巴擁有非常多的傳承
　　弟子，包括他的三個轉世化身：欽哲耶喜多傑（意化身）、巴楚仁波
　　切（語化身）和蔣揚欽哲旺波（身化身）。

說道：「噁！你腦袋瓜裡想著什麼邪惡、迂腐的念頭！你這條老狗！」接著朝巴楚臉上吐口水，向他伸小指（一種極端輕蔑的手勢），就走了。剎那間，巴楚了悟到：「我完全被迷惑了。這是一個直指究竟心性的甚深教授。」他以禪定姿坐下，無礙覺性（unobstructed awareness）的證量從心中自然生起，清朗如無雲晴空。早先吉美・嘉威・紐古授予的本覺教示宛如破曉，而多欽哲給他的這個證驗則像完整的日出。後來，巴楚仁波切開玩笑地說：「『老狗』是多欽哲給我的一個祕密灌頂法名。」在巴楚仁波切的一些著作上，他也署名為「老狗」。

在他前世的姪兒過世後，巴楚仁波切決定終其餘生過著無家、無恆產的生活。他將一切寺務料理妥當後，就離開過著浪遊的生活。

卓千寺[5]四周險峻、茂密的山丘及谷地，星布著棲身小屋和茅棚，是巴楚仁波切無家生活初期泰半的居住之地，往後

5　卓千寺（Dzogchen Monastery）：寧瑪巴六大主要寺廟之一，位於東藏康區德格，創建於西元 1685 年。在十八世紀初期，在該寺的建議之下，德格王建立了極為豐富的佛陀教法收藏，對於佛法的存續有很大的貢獻。同時，該寺也建立了許多閉關中心和佛教學院。

他也常回到那兒。在卓千寺，他從嘉瑟・賢遍・泰耶和成就者第四世卓千仁波切敏珠・南開・多傑（Mingyur Namkhai Dorje）處得到很多教授。他也在此處的大威德禪修洞（Yamantaka Meditation Cave）中寫下名著《普賢上師言教》[6]。

在山林間漫遊，住在山洞、森林與荒煙蔓草中的隱修處，他持續禪修著慈、悲和菩提心——願一切眾生解脫成佛。這些是他所持守的修行根本。對任何人，不論尊卑，他都會說：「沒有任何事比心地善良、行為仁慈更重要。」當他的菩提心愈趨深廣時，對於究竟當下的大圓滿證悟也就愈發深入。

四十三歲那年，巴楚仁波切前往安多（Amdo）拜會偉大的上師夏嘎・措竹・讓卓（Shabkar Tsokdruk Rangdrol）。在半路上，他聽說夏嘎已經圓寂，便改道去了果洛（Golok）。在那兒，他再度常伴嘉瑟・賢遍・泰耶。他教化了果洛地區

---

6 《普賢上師言教》（*The Words of My Perfect Teacher*）：作者為巴楚仁波切（1808~1887）是寧瑪巴的心意伏藏《龍欽心髓》的前行講義，一百多年來普遍被藏傳佛教四大門派用作心靈修持的指引。

的人民，甚至說服強盜與獵人放棄劫奪和殺生。

　　年輕時，他師事當時最偉大的上師，並以驚人的記性將學到的大部分法教牢記於心。稍長，他能一次教導最複雜的佛教哲理長達數月，毋須倚賴任何一頁經文。他說法時，人們的心完全被轉化。每位聆法者都感受到祥和，且能毫不費力地安住於思惟修。他所說的話，即使只有簡單數語，也能開啟一道通往修行生活、連綿不絕的新視野之門。他的開示直截了當，可讓人們立即應用於內在的修證經驗上。他淵博的學識、溫暖的加持力和深廣的內證功夫，使他的法教擁有迥異於其他上師的特質。

　　從他的外表、衣著以及和不相識者的相處方式來看，巴楚仁波切與一般人無異。偶然遇見他的人，都想不到他是一位偉大的上師。甚至還有一些不認識他的喇嘛，對他講授巴楚仁波切自己的著作。他一無所有，完全遠離俗務，也從不接受供養。如果有人堅持供養他一些金、銀或其他貴重物品，他便隨處放置，然後毫不在意地離開。當他停留於某地時，沒有固定的計畫；離開某地時，也不會有特定的目的地。他身上只帶著一根拐杖、隨身衣物，以及一只裝著煮茶用的泥壺與一本《入菩薩行論》[7]（Bodhicharyavatara）的小布袋。他隨意在森林、山洞或不知名的途中停歇，久暫不定。

　　每個與他相處過的人都說他只談論佛法。他可能會傳法，或述說古代偉大上師的故事，但從沒有人聽他聊過世俗的閒話。他幾乎不太講話，而開口時，都非常坦率直接，對那些喜好恭維的人來說是很不舒服的。他的風範令人敬畏，甚至在一開始令人感到害怕，也只有那些真心需要他的精神指引的人才會接近他。但所有堅持追隨他的人，到最後都會發現自己離不開他。

　　當今所有最優秀的上師們咸認巴楚仁波切是最傑出的禪修大師，毫無疑問地已證得了勝義諦[8]。至尊達賴喇嘛常公開讚美巴楚仁波切的菩提心教授，是他持守和傳授的法教。頂

7　《入菩薩行論》：寂天菩薩於八世紀所著，啟發修行者如何發菩提心、行大願力，突破人我法執，安住光明的空性之中。

8　勝義諦（AbsoluteTruth）：心的究竟本質，以及所有現象的真實狀態；這種狀態超越所有概念之造作和二元分立，唯有本初智慧才能了悟這種狀態。這是證悟者看待事物的方式。

果欽哲仁波切也推崇巴楚仁波切是修持大圓滿[9]見、修、行的完美典範。

　　巴楚仁波切確實從心裡了解十四世紀的大師嘉華‧龍欽巴（Gyalwa Longchenpa）著名的《七寶藏論》[10]（*Seven Treasures*）及其他作品，他認為嘉華‧龍欽巴是佛教修行道次第的究竟權威（ultimate authority）。當巴楚仁波切在山洞或簡陋的隱密處閉關時，會寫下一些作品；這些高深、原創的論釋大多收錄在他的六函著述中。他最受歡迎的作品《普賢上師言教》，是以鮮明的地方色彩穿插豐富軼聞的方式，來闡述吉美‧嘉威‧紐古傳授的寧瑪派傳統前行法（或加行法）。此書受到西藏各教派大師和弟子的一致推崇。

　　巴楚仁波切毫無偏私地教導各教派的弟子。他與蔣貢‧康楚‧羅卓‧泰耶（Jamgon Kongtrul Lodro Thaye）、蔣揚‧

9　大圓滿（Dzogchen）：寧瑪派所分「九乘」中的最高見地法門。第九乘，指的是一切現象原始即清淨，以及一切眾生內在任運天成的覺性特質，稱為「大圓滿」是因為所有的能量都包含在此本初的圓滿中。大圓滿有三大主要傳承：由蓮師所傳下的空行心髓，由毘瑪拉密扎所傳下的毘瑪心髓，以及由毘盧遮那所傳下的毘盧心髓。

10　《七寶藏論》（*Seven Treasuries*，*mdzod-bdun*）：由被尊稱為繼蓮花生大師之後的「第二佛」－龍欽巴尊者所著，是寧瑪巴最高心法大圓滿法的重要傳承依據。

欽哲‧旺波及米滂上師（Lama Mipham）在不分派運動
（nonsectarian movement）的發展中扮演了舉足輕重的角色。
此運動在十九世紀興起，當許多珍貴的傳承與法教瀕臨滅絕
時，曾重振了西藏的佛教。巴楚仁波切力倡獨處之樂與隱修
的簡樸生活，總是強調世俗的努力和追求是無益的。

　　一八八五年，巴楚仁波切七十七歲時，返回出生地札秋
喀，直到一八八七年圓寂。他的侍者蘇南‧才仁（Sonam
Tsering）描述了他圓寂前數小時的情形：

　　十七日當天，他吃了一點食物，並念誦懺悔續
（Confession Tantra）。然後做了一些大禮拜、五支瑜伽
（fivefold yogic exercise）和運動來打開心脈。翌日清晨，他
吃了一些酸奶，喝了一些茶。當陽光開始普照時，他脫掉衣
服，身體坐直，盤腿金剛坐，雙手置於膝上。當我替他披上
衣服時，他沒有說什麼。當時有三個人在他身邊——貢陽
（Kungyam）、醫師和我。一段時間後，他兩眼直視虛空，雙
手手指輕扣在衣服下結定印，然後進入廣大光明的內在本淨
虛空中（inner space of primordial purity），圓寂的無上圓滿境
界。

　　巴楚仁波切的諸多重要弟子包括第三世多竹千仁波切
（Dodrupchen Rinpoche）、紐修・隆多・滇貝・尼瑪
（Nyoshul Lungthok Tenpai Nyima）、阿宗・竹巴（Adzom
Drukpa）、米滂仁波切、掘藏師索甲（Terton Sogyal）、第五
世卓千仁波切（Dzogchen Rinpoche）、第二世噶陀・錫度仁
波切（Katok Situ Rinpoche）、堪布昆桑・巴登（Khenpo
Kunzang Pelden）、堪布雍嘎（Khenpo Yonga）以及堪布賢嘎
（Khenpo Shenga）。現今很多偉大上師持有巴楚仁波切法教
的直接傳承，其間只隔了一、兩代。頂果欽哲仁波切幼年曾
受米滂仁波切加持，並從巴楚仁波切的幾位親傳弟子處領受
法教。因此巴楚仁波切的法教、加持及啟迪力，至今仍與我
們同在。

　　＊本篇簡傳引用自頂果欽哲法王著作《唵嘛呢唄美吽》
　　一書。

〔**導讀**〕

　　本書作者巴楚仁波切（Patrul Rinpoche），是寧瑪派最偉大的禪修大師和作家。

　　第一世多竹‧千仁波切為巴楚仁波切命名為吉美‧卻吉‧旺波。西元一八〇八年，他出生於札秋喀地區的一個遊牧部族，並且被多拉‧吉美‧卡桑認證為卓千寺的巴給轉世。

　　他師事西藏東部偉大的聖者和學者：吉美‧卡桑、吉美‧哦夏、嘉瑟‧賢遍‧泰耶和第四世卓千仁波切等人，學習西藏所有佛教傳承的智慧。尤其從吉美‧嘉威‧紐古和多‧欽哲‧耶喜‧多傑那裡，領受了傳承的智慧與證悟口傳。他從吉美‧嘉威‧紐古那裡，領受了二十五次的《龍欽心髓》前行解說。當他放棄寺院的義務，成為一名隱士之後，在果洛地區漫遊，用佛法調伏果洛地區粗暴的部族，使佛法繁榮興盛。他不只接觸學者、興建佛學院，也接近連學習簡單祈願文的機會都沒有的人，教導他們如何念誦六字大明咒，並投入數年時間資助和監督建造一堵巨大的石牆，上面寫有十萬遍的六字大明咒。他在卓千寺著名的師利星哈佛學院、蓮花院、那瓊閉關中心和其它機構教授佛經。最後，他在家鄉部落札秋喀地區美麗廣大的游牧草原上度過晚年。西元一八八七年火豬年的四月十八日，巴楚仁波切圓寂，融入究竟自性之中。

　　巴楚仁波切針對各種不同主題撰寫了六函論著，包括哲學、詩歌、倫理學和密教教法（密續）。在西藏東部，他或許是最關鍵的人物，把《入菩薩行論》變成眾多僧人使用的手冊；把《投生極樂淨土祈願文》變成許多在家人每日念誦的祈願文；把《幻網續》（也稱做《秘密藏續》）變成寧瑪傳承的基石；把大圓滿教法變成不僅是典籍傳承也是活生生的修持，尤其是把六字大明咒變成恆久的呼息。

　　這本小冊子是針對各種年齡層，尤其是年輕人所寫的倫常忠告。作者以一位年輕人和一位老人之間的對話形式來撰寫。這個年輕人充滿驕慢，輕蔑他人。那個老人經驗豐富、性情柔和、充滿智慧，他告訴年輕人，當他年輕時，比年輕人更聰穎傑出。這席話讓年輕人感到震驚。

　　當我年輕力壯時，
　　我比你更聰穎。
　　當我擁有家園和故土時，
　　我比你更傑出。

　　然後,老人讓年輕人平靜下來,領著他狂野的心進入道德倫常的優美之中。仁波切在文中清楚地指出,我沒有必要班門弄斧地談論修行倫常,所以現在扼要地告訴你一些世俗倫常。然而,因為作者本身的倫理背景和西藏的文化,所有的忠告都基於或受到佛教用語和價值的影響。

　　因此,從佛教智慧的角度來看,本書可以被歸類為世俗倫常的忠告。作者使用許多東藏部族風行和討喜的俗諺,也引用佛教的格言來說明、支持他的見解。就今日來說,書中揭示的問題,在我們生活中處處可見。如果,書中的忠告觸動了你的心靈,別只是觸動,請將之銘記在心,並在生活中徹底實踐。

西藏東部多美（Dome）省著名的札摩林嘎朵（Thramo Lingkar Tod）地區，有一戶人家的兒子名叫宗努洛登（Zhonnu Loden）。他天資聰穎，秉性良善，具備一個溫柔者的所有善巧。但是他在幼年時期即父母雙亡，沒有人給他良好的忠告，因而結交了損友，從事諸如偷盜、欺瞞等粗魯的行徑。有一天，他走在路上，遇見一個白髮蒼蒼的白鬚老人拄著拐杖，步履蹣跚地行走。宗努洛登看著老人，邊笑邊說：

In the famous Thramo Lingkar Tod [Khra-Mo Gling-dKar sTod] in the province of Dome [mDo- sMad; in eastern Tibet] there lived a family with a son named Zhonnu Loden [gZon-Nu Blo lDan]. He was bright, good nature, and had all the skills of a gentle person. But because his parents died when he was young, he had no one to give him good advice; so he fell in with bad companions. He became involved in crude behavior such as stealing, lying, and cheating. One day while he was walking along a road, he met an old man with white beard and white hair, holding a walking stick and moving along with doddering steps. Looking at the old man, the boy laughed and said:

哈！哈！沒有冬霜，
所以你不必戴著羊皮帽。
沒有惡犬，
所以你不必拿著柳杖。
這裡沒有跳舞的地方，
所以你不必踏著搖搖擺擺的步子。
老人，你屬於何處？
今晨你來自何處？
今晚你要去何處？
給我一個直截了當的回答，
不要有所隱瞞。

Ha ! Ha !There's no winter frost,

So you don't have to put on a lambskin hat.

There's no fierce dog,

So you don't have to carry a willow stick.

There's no place to dance here,

So you don't have to take tottering steps.

Old man, which place do you belong to ?

Where are you coming from this morning ?

Where are you going tonight ?

Give me a straight answer and don't hide anything.

老人瞪大眼睛對著男孩說：

哈！哈！從你輕蔑、趾高氣昂的樣子看來，
你似乎年輕而驕慢。
你詼諧地取笑和吹噓，
讓自己看起來聰穎卻舉止惡劣。
從你譏諷一個老人的樣子看來，
你似乎沒有父母，只有損友。
海可枯，石可爛，
甚至連幼虎的光澤皮毛也會失色。
一個父親會生出好兒子和不肖子。
我年輕力壯時，比你聰穎。
我擁有家園和故土時，比你更傑出。

Then the old man stared with wide open eyes at the boy

and said :

Ha ! Ha !From the way you strut scornfully,

You seem to be young and proud.

Your witty style of joking and boasting,

Makes you out to be clever but ill-mannered.

From your sarcasm toward an old man,

It seems you have no parents, only bad friends.

Old age comes even to solid rocks.

Even the glossy fur of the youthful tiger fades.

There are good and bad sons of the same father.

When I had the flesh and blood of youth,

I was brighter than you.

When I had my own home and country,

I was more distinguished than you.

我來自多康（Do Kham）省，

今晨我來自輪迴[1]城，

今晚要前往解脫[2]島。

年輕的男孩心想：「聽他說話的樣子，似乎是一個博學多聞的老者。」他對老人說：「嘿，老人家，在這坐一會兒，告訴我一些事情。」

老人回答：「我該說些什麼？我不知道如何談論佛法[3]。你不會聽從世俗的忠告。我還是走我的路比較好。」

年輕男孩應允地說：「你說什麼我都會聽從。」

---

1 輪迴（Samsara）：生、死與再生的不斷循環，其間充滿苦痛，今生只不過是個瞬間。唯有當一個人了悟現象的空性，才能去除心之障蔽，從輪迴中解脫。

2 解脫（Liberation）：離於痛苦和輪迴，但是解脫仍然不是獲得完全證悟的狀態。

3 佛法（Dharma）：這個梵文詞彙一般是指佛陀的法教。「教法」（Dharma of transmission）是指所有實際傳授的法教，不論是口語的或書寫的。「證法」（Dharma of realization）是指從實修這些法教所獲得的心靈品德。

I am from Do Kham province.

This morning I came from the City of

Samsara.

Tonight I am going to the Island of Liberation.

The young boy thought, "To hear him talk this way, he seems like a learned old man." He said to him, "Hey, old man, sit here a while and tell me something."

The old man replied, "What shall I say ? I don't know how to speak about Dharma. You won't listen to worldly advice. Better for an old man to go on his way."

The young boy promised, saying, "I really will listen to whatever you say."

　　於是老人慢慢地坐下，說：「喔，我沒有學問去說太多佛法或談論這個世界——即使我知道在這個晦暗的時代，所有人都在依循粗魯而有害的行為，懷著自私自利、狡猾奸詐的念頭虛度光陰，他們心懷惡意，以邪曲的方式行事。這是一個隱善揚惡的時代，這是一個無恥而非誠實者當道的時代，這是一個喜新友厭舊恩的時代。如今，君主的統御紊亂無章，臣民的舉止混亂失序。人們忘卻來生，讚揚崇拜無恥愚蠢者的行為。如果有人尋求良善行為的忠告，人們不但認為這是愚蠢的，許多人甚至不曉得他們要學習世間倫常。在這個邪惡的時代，像我這樣的人說話是毫無用處的。但是如諺語所說：

Then the old man slowly sat down and said, "Oh, I don't have the knowledge to say much about the Dharma or the world-- even though I know that all the people of this dull age are following a way of crude and evil conduct, and are just passing their time with selfish and cunning thoughts; that they harbor only thoughts of ill-will and are acting in perverted ways. This is the age of popularity of the bad rather than the good, the age of victory for shameless rather than honest people, the age of preferring new friends over those to whom we owe gratitude. Now the rule of the higher authorities is chaotic and the behaviors of the subjects in disorder. Forgetting about the next life, people praise and heroize the activities of men who are shameless and stupid. And if someone seeks advice about good conduct, not only do people think it foolish, but many are not even aware that there are worldly ethics to be learned. In this evil age, it is useless for a man like me to speak. But as a proverb has it:

朋友提問時，除了談論之外別無選擇。

殘忍的人掌摑狐狸的臉頰時，

狐狸除了叫喊之外別無選擇。

犬隻看見黑影時，牠們不得不吠叫。

因此，既然你問我，我就應該告訴你。俗話說：

如果有人詢問，就應該加以告知；

如果一個人要學習，就應該受教。」

There is no choice but to do much talking when questioned
by a friend.

Foxes have no choice but to yelp when the demous slap their
cheeks !

Dogs can't help barking when they see a dark shadow.

So, since you ask me, I should tell you, The saying goes:

If asked, one should tell;
If a man studies, he should be taught."

　　「現在，我簡短地告訴你修行的倫常。第一，修行倫常的老師是善知識，也就是喇嘛[4]。而佛陀的教誨是其來源。第二，人們應該修持懺悔，生起菩提心[5]、淨見[6]、禪定[7]等等，這些是別解脫戒、菩薩戒和密乘戒[8]的根本，適用於具有下等、中等和上等根器的修行者。最後，盡除吾人自心染污的根本，是獲致證悟[9]。此乃一切聖教法門的精髓。」

4　喇嘛（Lama）：(1) 上師，是「無上」（bla na med pa）這個字的簡稱；
　　(2) 常被用來泛稱藏傳佛教僧侶或瑜珈士。

5　菩提心（Bodhichitta）：字面意義為「證悟之心」。在相對的層面，菩提心是指為了一切眾生而證悟成佛的願望，以及為了達到這個目的所做之修行。在究竟的層面上，菩提心是指對自我與現象究竟本性的直觀。

6　淨見：非二元、無染污的見解。

7　禪定：透過以修持穩定的「止」為基礎，開展出深度的「觀」，煩惱能夠完全被降服。在止與觀之中，觀是最重要的，但沒有修止的心，觀就無法生起。

8　三種誓戒：

(1) 別解脫戒：佛陀在律部中教導在家眾及出家眾有關行為的訓誡。

(2) 菩薩戒：就是發誓要將自己的念頭、語言及行為全然奉獻予利益他人，同時希望能生起、培養及保存這個誓願；相對而言，這指的是慈愛、悲憫及六度的修習，最終是引領一切眾生全然覺醒。

(3) 密乘戒（三昧耶戒）：當弟子事奉心靈導師及從上師處接受灌頂時，所創造出來的神聖聯繫。雖然有人說在密咒乘中有十萬種三昧耶誓言，但它們能濃縮為與上師身、語、意相關的誓言。

9　證悟（Enlightenment）：成佛（Buddhahood）的同義字，修行的究竟成就，圓滿的內在智慧結合了無限的悲心。圓滿了悟心和現象的究竟本質，也就是這兩者的相對存在（其表象）和絕對自性（其本質）；這樣的了悟是對治無明的重要解藥，因此也是對治痛苦的解藥。

"Now, to tell you briefly about spiritual ethics: First, the teacher of spiritual ethics is the virtuous friend, the lama. And the source is the Buddha's docrine. Second, one should practice repentance, develop Bodhi mind, pure view, meditation, and so on, which are the roots of the Pratimoksa, Bodhisattva, and tantric disciplines, appropriate to the lesser, medium, and high intelligence of individual minds. Finally, the elimination of the roots of defilement of one's own mind is the attainment of enlightenment. This is the condensation of the methods of all holy doctrines."

「關於世俗倫常,第一,父母和長輩是世俗倫常的老師,而君王、大臣和古代菩薩的道德著作則是世俗倫常的源頭。第二,所有的君王和百姓,上位者和下位者、富者和貧者等不同階級地位的人,都應該依照敬重上位者、服務下位者、結交同等地位者的倫理道德來行止。最後,踏上通往今生安樂與來世解脫的道路,乃是世俗倫常的精髓。」

「至於修行倫常,有數不盡的經書、釋論、著述和教訣加以說明,因此我沒有必要班門弄斧地談論修行倫常。所以我現在應該簡短地告訴你一些世俗倫常。」

"About worldly ethics: First, the teachers of worldly ethics are the parents and the older generation. And the source is the ethical writings of the holy kings, ministers, and Bodhisattvas of ancient times. Second, all kings, ministers, and subjects, the higher and the lower, the rich and the poor, in proportion to their degrees, should act according to the ethic of respecting the higher, serving the lower, and associating with equals. Finally, to set out on the path that leads to happiness in this life and to Liberation in the next is the condensation of worldly ethics."

"As for spiritual ethics, there are endless cononical scriptures and commentaries, texts, and instructions; so it is not necessary for me to muddle along trying to talk about them. So now I shall tell you about worldly ethics in brief."

世俗倫常：
敬重上位者的道德倫常

「對於那些上位者或下位者、善良者或邪惡者而言，今生、來世的希望根源和支持對象，莫過於三寶[10]。因此，人們應該懷著專一的信心，尊重禮敬、頂禮和供養（代表諸佛、菩薩、和聖眾之）身、語、意的對象，例如佛像、經典和佛塔，不論這些對象新舊或品質良莠。因為，如《入菩薩行論》（Bodhicharyavatara）所說：

生起虔敬心者，
聖者（佛）將在其面前示顯。」

10　三寶（Three Jewels）：佛、法與僧。

WORLDLY ETHICS

THE ETHIC OF RESPECT FOR SUPERIORS

"For those who are higher or lower, good or bad, there is no source of hope or object of support in this life or the next other than the Three Jewels. Therefore, one should pay respect and homage, and make offerings with one-pointed faith to the objects of the Body, Speech, and Mind [of the Buddhas, Bodhi sattvas, and Sages], such as images, holy scriptures, and stupas, whether they are old or new or of good or bad quality. For, as it is said [in the *Bodhicharyavatara*]:

Whoever develops devotion,

The Sage [Buddha] will be present before him".

「對喇嘛、僧侶和虔誠的人沒有信心、批評或輕蔑他們美好或粗劣品質，尤其不恰當。因為他們是死者心識的守護者；生者尋求保護的對象；有供品者行供養的對象；以及沒有供品者祈請的對象。在這個世界上，沒有什麼比三寶更為殊勝了。如果人們對三寶表現出一點點信心和虔敬或累積功德，或如果人們批評三寶或對三寶心懷惡意，其結果將難以想像。像我們這樣的人無法分辨三寶的良莠品質。世尊佛陀說：

除了我或像我的人之外，人們去評斷他人是不恰當的。」

"It is especially improper to be faithless, critical, or contemptuous of the good and bad qualities of lamas, monks, and religious persons. For they are the custodians of the consciousness of the dead, the objects of requests for protection by the living, the objects of offerings for those who have, and the objects of supplication for those who have not. In this world there is no more sacred object than the Three Jewels. If one performs a small act of faith and devotion to them or accumulates merit, or if one speaks critically or with ill-will of the Three Jewels, the results will be unimaginable. Their good and bad qualities cannot be distinguished by men like us. The gracious Buddha said:

Except by me or one like me, it is not proper for
men to be judged by men."

「即使當人們認為某些事物是不淨的，也應該生起淨[11]觀和虔敬心。不要讓自己墮落，如此，他人的過失將不會對你造成傷害。在修行倫常和世俗倫常之中，沒有比找出他人的過失並加以毀謗、中傷更為嚴重的過患了。」

那不是他人的過失，而是自己的過失──
就如同鏡面所現出的反影。

「如果你在某人面前數落另一個人的過失，又如果那個人是個深思熟慮的人，那麼他可能表面上附和你，但事實上，卻對你的行為感到厭惡。因為從你說話的方式，他可能認為你是個雙面人。因此話說：

11　淨觀：是超越了世俗、二元概念的限制，能直觀到現象本性、空性的修行成就。

"Even when one perceives some seeming impurity, one should develop pure perception and devotion. Do not allow yourself to degenerate, and the faults of others will not harm you. There is no more serious fault either in spiritual or in worldly ethics than trying to find the faults of others and defaming them."

It is not the faults of others. But one's own faults-
Like reflections rising in the surface of a morror.

"If you tell someone the faults of another, and if he is a thoughtful person, he may appear to agree with you, but actually he will disgust to you. For he may think by the way you're talking that you are two- faced. So it is said:

不要去想他人的過失，而去想你自己的過失；
不要去挖掘任何人的惡行，而去挖掘你自己的惡行。」

「你應該對所有的首領、君王、大臣、領袖、舉國的長者、父母、老師和善知識顯示敬重，替他們開門、安排座位，歡迎他們，替他們送行，對他們表現出信心和恭敬，行為舉止要謙遜、謹慎。今日，一些人自認地位崇高、博學或富有而藐視其他人。事實上，這麼做暴露了自身的過患，證明他們既沒有修行，也沒有世俗的善德。例如話說：

Do not think of other's faults but of your own;

Do not dig up anyone's misdeeds but your own."

"In your behavior toward all the chieftains, kings, ministers, leaders, the older generations of the country, parents, teachers, and spiritual friends, you should show respect, open the doors for them, arrange their seats, welcome them, see them off, show them faith and respect, and conduct yourself humble and circumspectly. Nowadays, some people, considering themselves high or scholarly or rich, show contempt for everybody else. Actually, in doing so their own faults are exposed, proving that they possess neither spiritual nor worldly virtues. For example, it is said:

沒有善德者將驕傲自大，
穀穗空虛者將昂首挺立。

又說：

善德之水將不會停留在驕慢的頂峰之上。」

「在西藏，沒有人比赤松德贊王[12]更有權力、更富有、更良善，但是他卻敬重一個過得像乞丐的瑜伽士[13]，並且在他的跟前行大禮拜[14]。對其他人，赤松德贊則施行十六淨行律儀[15]（Sixteen Principles of Pure Human Conduct）。因此你應該見賢思齊，並為未來提供良好的示範，那些有教養者將擁有柔和的天性、誠實的性情和寬廣的心胸。」

12　赤松德贊王：（Trisong Detsen，790~844）西藏國王，崇信佛教，曾邀請印度蓮花生大士等人入藏，翻譯了大量的佛經，也促成了密教在西藏的扎根，被尊為護教法王。

13　瑜伽士：「瑜伽」一詞藏文的意義為相應，是對過著流浪刻苦生活的禪修者，或戒律嚴持的出家人等的一種讚嘆與敬稱。現在也可成為對在家修行人的稱呼。

14　大禮拜：正式的大禮拜，也被稱為虔誠之大禮拜，是全身手腳伸展開，撲倒在地上，這帶來更大的利益及更迅速的淨化。屬於身、語、意中，身部分的修行，也是四不共前行的第一個前行。

15　律儀：律是戒律，儀是儀則，謂佛所制定的戒律可以使人防非止惡，乃是吾人立身處世的儀則。

Those without virtues will have great pride,

Empty husks will hold their heads high.

And:

On the peak of pride the water of virtue will not stay."

"Tibet never had a man who had more power, riches, and goodness than Chogyal Thrisong Detsen [790-844]. Yet he showed respect to and prostrated himself before a yogi who lived like a beggar. For others he enacted a law of Sixteen Principles of Pure Human Conduct. So you should look up to your superiors and provide good examples for the future. Thus, those who are cultivated will have gentle nature, honest disposition, and a broad mind."

服務一般人的道德倫常

「你不應該輕視、仇恨或虐待比你弱、比你更無助、比你更貧窮、或比你更乞討的人。你應該努力提供他們所有的利益，不管是言語的、食物的或衣服的利益。無法幫助他們的時候，你應該有禮貌且誠實。以武力、威脅或暴力來對抗比較弱勢的人，並且假裝自己勇敢，是一種自我毀滅的行為。因此話說：

對隻手鋒利的刀是惡刀，

對乞丐兇猛的狗是惡犬，

對弱者發怒的人是惡人。

又說：

如果你希望居於高位，就要採取較低的位置；

如果你希望勝利，就必須接受失敗。」

THEETHIC OF SERVICE TO ORDINARY PEOPLE

"You should not have contempt, hatred, or abuse those who are weaker, more helpless, poorer, or more beggarly than you. And you should try to provide them with all the benefits of speech, food, or cholthes. In the event that you cannot help them you should be polite and honest. The use of force, threats, or violence against weaker people and pretending to be a brave man is self-destructive. So it is said:

A bad knife is sharp to the hand,
A bad dog is fierce to beggars,
A bad man is wrathful to the weak.

And:

If you wish to be high, take the lower place;
If you want victory, you must accept defeat."

「看見一點點他人的財富、地位和權勢，驚訝地遮掩嘴
巴；看見弱者、乞丐和不幸的人，趾高氣昂地輕視他們；為
小事而興奮雀躍——這是對幸運、厄運，或對世間苦、樂沒
有任何體驗的徵兆。不論你看到什麼，上或下、好或壞，你
都不應該過於喜愛上位者，或過於厭惡下位者，因為痛苦與
快樂、好與壞都會發生在你身上。上位或下位、快樂或悲
傷、富裕或貧困維持一輩子，是罕見的。如話說：

　　維持長久的和諧是罕見的；
　　富人終身快樂是罕見的；
　　學者從未犯錯是罕見的。」

"Seeing the bit of wealth, position, and power of others, and covering one's mouth with astonishment; seeing the weak, beggars, and miserable people, and looking down on them with one's nose in the air; getting excited over little things- these are signs of not having any experience of high and low fortune or of the happiness and suffeiring of the world. Whatever you see, high or low, good or bad, you should not be too fond of the high nor too repelled by the low, because happiness and sorrow, good and bad, will happen to you. It is rare for high or low position, happiness or sorrow, riches or poverty to last for a whole life time. As it is said:

> It is rare to maintain harmony for a long time;
> It is rare for a rich man to be happy for his whole life;
> It is rare for a scholar never to make a mistake."

與同輩相處的道德倫常

　　「對於親戚、朋友、同胞和鄰居，絕對不應該偷盜、欺瞞、製造不和、厚顏無恥或不可靠、背後中傷毀謗、嘲笑或辱罵。你應該竭盡所能利益他們。你不應該對他們所做的細小行為動輒感到高興或不悅。你應該要能忍受快樂和不悅，並為自己留有面對好、壞偶發事件的空間。你不應該想到什麼就做什麼，相反的，你要穩定而專心。你應該和所有人和諧相處，並且不失謙遜。

THE ETHIC OF ASSOCIATION WITH EQUALS

"In relation to your relatives, friends, countrymen, and neighbors you should never steal, lie, cheat, create discord, be shameless or untrustworthy, backbite, deride, or abuse. You should try to do for all of them whatever you can and is beneficial. And you should not be quick to feel happiness or unhappiness over slight actions of theirs. You should be able to bear happiness and unhappiness and have room in yourself for good and bad eventualities. You should not get involved in doing everything that comes into your mind. Instead, be stable and single-minded. You should be harmonious with everyone, and not lose your modesty.

　　將心比心、易地而處地檢視情況是重要的。不論你是誰，都應該認清自己的過失。人們有尖銳的指針指出別人的過錯，但是極少人有一面鏡子看清自己的過失。如果你不檢視自己，沒有人會指出你的過失。人們可能在你的面前諂媚，卻在你背後誹謗中傷。人們懷著好意、坦率直接地揭露他人的過失，而非言聽計從的時候，後者會認為前者懷有敵意。如話說：

It is important to examine situations by putting others in your position and yourself in the position of others. Whoever you are, you should recognize your own faults. People have a sharp pointer for showing other's faults, but it is very rare for them to have a mirror in which to see their own. If you do not examine yourself, there will be no one who will point them out to you. People may flatter you to your face, but behind your back there will be only backbiting and detraction. When people's faults are revealed to them straightforwardly with good intentions, rather than listen to they will treat it as enmity. As it is said:

有罪者發怒；

背部有傷口的馬匹暴跳。」

「這年頭，人們認為自己完美無缺，但是你應該研習學者所著的道德典籍，觀察你的天性來改革自己的心。你懂嗎？」

宗努洛登說：「好的，那是面對上位者、同輩和下位者的方式。但是這年頭，即使我們安分守己，從事眾多勤務，許多人，例如首領，仍然會因為我們所犯下的輕罪而用毆打、沒收財物等方式，嚴厲地懲罰我們。如乞丐等下位者、如親戚朋友等同輩也是如此，即使我們盡可能地幫助他們，彷彿是自己親生的兒子，他們仍有許多人待我們如敵人，竊取我們的財富，搶奪我們的妻子，並且欺騙我們。告訴我，我們應該怎麼做？」

A guilty man gets angry;

A horse with sores on its back rears up."

"Nowadays people consider themselves perfect, but you should reform your mind by studying the ethical scriptures of scholars and watching your own nature, do you understand ?"

Then Zhonnu Loden said, "All right, that is the way to deal with higher, middling, and lower people. But nowadays many people, such as chieftains, will punish us severely with beatings and confiscation for a small misdemeanor, even if we have always been obedient and performed many services. Also, in the case of lower people like beggars and middling people like relatives and friend, even if we help them as much as we can, as though they were our own son ; many of them treat us like enemies by stealing our wealth, snatching our wives, and cheating us. So tell me, what should we do ?"

　　於是老人說：「喔，聰明的小子！你這麼深思熟慮地提出問題是好的，因為光是聽聞很難理解。首先，不論人們的地位崇高、同等或低賤，你應該考慮他們的品質。在他們之中，有上等、中等和下等之別。上等者會服務國家人民，他自身的權益和興趣會自動達成。中等者會在沒有傷害他人的情況下實現願望。下等者會傷害他人試圖滿足自身的利益，但很難如願以償。在某些情況下，心懷惡意的人會寡廉鮮恥、無所不用其極地達成自身的利益。他們可能會實現部分的目標，但是會受到他人的中傷誹謗。在每個類別的人之中，有三種層次的品質。而根據修行的和世俗的倫常，也有三種分類。」

Then the old man said, "Oh, intelligent boy ! It is good that you ask in such a thoughtful way. For it is difficult to understand just by listening. First, you should consider the qualities of people, regardless of whether they are of high, middle, or low rank. Among them are the excellent, the mediocre, and the inferior. The excellent person will work for the country and the people, and his own interests will automatically be achieved. Without harming others, mediocre people will achieve their wishes. Inferior people will attempt to satisfy only their own interests by harming others, but still will be difficult for them to achieve what they want. But in some cases vicious people will struggle persistently to achieve their own self-interest, suppressing all modesty or shame. They may partially accomplish their aims, but then they will be defamed by others. In each category there are three levels of qualities. And also there are three classifications according to both spiritual and worldly ethics."

「今天，人們讚揚一個人的時候，可以把那個人捧上天；批評一個人的時候，可以把那個人打入地底。人們不知道如何行止得宜。這是心胸狹窄的過失。話說：

不要太快讚美一個陌生人；
不要太快對朋友表達快樂或不悅。」

「即使是優秀的喇嘛和首領，也會有一些不善的品質。即使是小偷、乞丐等惡人中，也會擁有美好品質之人。但是我們必須找出哪些人具有比較多的美好品質，哪些人有比較多不善的品質。話說：

"Nowadays when someone is praised, it raises him to the middle of the blue sky; and if someone is criticized, it drives him down under the deep earth. People don't know how to assign things their rightful place. This is the fault of narrow-minded. It is said:

Do not praise an unknown person too soon;

Do not express happiness or unhappiness to a friend too soon."

"Even excellent lamas and chieftains will have some bad qualities. Even among bad people like thieves and beggars there will be no one who does not have a good quality. But we have to find out who has more good qualities and who has more bad. It is said:

具有美好品質而沒有粗劣品質的人是稀有的；

長得挺直而沒有節瘤的樹木是罕見的；

經過鍛鍊的鐵既銳利又柔韌是稀有的。」

「我們難以理解一個學者的心意、一個狡猾人的把戲，以及一個偽裝天性之人的本性。因此，你應該用各種方法，直接或間接地檢視人們。」

如果你知道如何檢視所發生的一切，

這個經驗將讓你感到快樂；

如果你知道如何檢視自己所學的一切，

這種熟稔將讓你感到快樂。

「如果你不這麼嚴密地檢視事物，你將難以有所理解。」

A man who has good qualities but no bad ones is rare;

A tree that has grown up straight with no gnarl is rare;

Tempered iron, sharp and flexible, is rare."

"It is difficult to understand the mind of a scholar, the game of a cunning person, and the nature of a man who disguises it. So you should examine people by various methods, directly of indirectly."

If you know how to examine whatever happens,

this experience will make you happy;

If you know haw to examine whatever you learn,

this familiarity will make you happy.

"If you don't examine things meticulously like that, it will be diffecult to gain understanding."

　　如果你不遭遇敵人和惡魔，

　　任何人都可能是自足的。

　　如果事不關乎財產或勞力，

　　任何人都可以慷慨陳詞。

　　如果你沒有身陷訴訟，

　　任何人都可以是滔滔雄辯的。

　　如果你不必面對嚴重的情況，

　　任何人都可以在他母親的廚房內做一個好人。

　　「人們應該謹慎地考量是非對錯，而不要匆促地下決定。」

　　「包括高階官員在內的領導人應該寡言、心胸開闊、獨立、立意良善和小心謹慎。尤其在賦稅和司法方面，他們不應該重視自身的權益，或受到財富和位階的左右，而應該樹立誠實行止的典範。」

If you don't encounter enemies and demons,

Anybody can be self-reliant.

If it is not a matter of property or labor,

Anybody can talk generously.

If you don't get caught in a lawsuit,

Anybody can be eloquent.

If you don't have to face a serious situation,

Anybody can be a good person in his mother's kitchen.

"One should carefully consider what is right or wrong without deciding hastily."

"Leaders, including officials of high rank, should be of few words, broad-minded, independent, well-intented, and metuculous. Especially in matters of taxes and justice, they should not cherish their own interests or be influenced by wealth and rank, but be examples of honest conduct."

如果沒有統治者，誰將拯救百姓？

如果沒有百姓，統治者將治理誰？

如果統治者誠實，統治者和百姓都將安樂強壯。

如果百姓富裕繁盛，那是王權的莊嚴。

好的統治者將照顧其百姓的福祉。

好的百姓將敬重其統治者。

如果木頭抬起木頭，那是棟與樑；

如果人抬舉人，那是主人與侍從。

If there is no ruler, who will save the head of subjects ?

If there are no subjects, whom shall the ruler govern ?

If the ruler is honest, both ruler and subjects will be happy and strong.

If the subjects prosper, that is the ornament of kingship.

Good rulers will look after the welfare of their subjects.

Good subjects will act respectfully to the ruler.

If wood elevates wood, that is a pillar and beam;

If a man elevates another, that is a servant and master.

「統治者與百姓應該像父子般相互支持。長輩、父親和伯叔應該寡言，並且文雅柔和。他們不應該把債務和訴訟等問題留給兒孫，應該愜意安樂地過活，修持正法來準備死亡。男人的思想和行為應該溫和穩健。他們應該能夠挺身面對強敵，和親戚、下屬討論時，應該有耐心。他們應該具有溫和的本性和經久的友誼，不應該喪失自持。」

如果兄弟鬩牆，厚顏無恥者將會獲勝。

同樣的，即使一個人在擊退外敵時充滿勇氣，

只有能夠接受自己被親戚擊敗，

他才算是一個好人。

"The ruler and subjects should support one another like father and son. The older generation, fathers and uncles, should be sparing in speech and gentle. They should not leave problems like debts and lawsuits for their sons and grandsons. They should live comfortably and happily, practice the pure Dharma in preparation for death. Men should be moderate in thought and action. They should be able to stand up to strong enemies. They should be patient in discussions with relatives and inferiors. They should have gentle natures and durable friendships. They should never lose their self-reliance."

If there is fighting among brothers, the shameless one will win.

Likewise, even if one is brave in defeating external enemies,

Only if he can accept defeat from his own relatives is he a good man.

「女人應該沉穩，不應該說長道短。她們應該把自己的丈夫視為天神，把其他人的丈夫當做毒藥般規避。她們應該整潔優雅，精於儲蓄，關心侍者和動物，謙遜端莊。」

「諸如侍者等部屬不應該懷有邪惡狡猾的念頭，不應該欺騙或偷盜、背後中傷或製造敵意。侍者應該忠於主人，不論大事小事，都要對主人言聽計從。不論人的位階高低，都不應該心懷惡意、狡猾、不穩定、太多話、不知節制或脾氣暴躁。」

沒有憤怒的朋友，是愉悅的。
沒有長滿蝨子的衣物，是舒適的。

「一般而言，對一個人好的事物，不會對每個人都好；對一個人壞的事物，不會對每個人都壞。會這樣，是因為個人不同的業果[16]。」

16　業（Karma）：梵文意指「行為」，指與我們的身、語、意相關的因果法則。根據佛陀的法教，眾生的命運、安樂、痛苦，以及對世界的看法，既不是機緣運氣的結果，也不是出自全能存在者的意志，它們都是先前行為的結果；同樣地，眾生的未來取決於他們目前所從事之行為的善惡。業也區分為共業和不共業，共業是指我們對周遭世界的一般看法，不共業則決定我們個人的經驗。

"Women should be mentally calm and should not gossip a lot. They should regard their own husbands as divine and shun other's husbands as poison. They should be neat, good at saving, caring toward the servants and animals, humble, and modest.

"Subordinates, such as servants, should not have evil or cunning thoughts, lie or steal, backbite, or create enmity. A servant should be devoted to his master and listen to whatever he says, whether it is a large or small matter. Whatever his rank, high, middle, or low, a person should not be evil-minded, cunning, unstable, overly talkative, immoderate, or hot tempered."

It is pleasant if you have no angry friend.
It is comfortable if you have no lice-ridden clothes.

"In general what is good for one person will not be good for everybody, and what is bad for one person will not be bad for everybody. This is so because of the various results of the karma of individuals."

「至於敵人，某些人成為敵人，是前業之果，其他是因為對他們的對手欠缺了解，另一些則是因為沒有選擇。此外，某些人成為敵人，是因為其他人製造不和之故，或是因為拙劣的評斷。如果敵人是一個有教養、能夠交往的人，你應該用友善的話語來平靜他的心，用善巧方便把他化敵為友。這種舉止是博學多聞者的行止。然而，如果敵人粗劣殘忍，你應該用溫柔語、堅韌的心和各種聰明的方法來征服他。用力量來降伏他是常見的方法。做出承諾但卻食言是愚蠢的。」

不知道怎麼說話，最好默不作聲。

無法完成的工作，最好不要開始。

無法達成的英勇行為，最好不要承擔。

"Concerning enemies, some become enemies because of previous karma, others because of lack of understanding of their opponents, others because there was no alternative. Again, some become enemies because of discord created by others. or because of poor judgment. In the case of an enemy who is a cultivated person and is capable of friendship, you should calm his mind with friendly words and win him over as a friend by skillful means. Such are the behaviors of learned people. If, However, the enemy is a bad or crude type of person, you should overcome him by gentle speech, a tough mind, and various clever methods. To subdue him forcefully by strength is the common way. Making promises without being able to keep them is foolish."

If you don't know how to speak, it's better to keep quiet.

Work that you cannot accomplish is better not started.

Brave deeds that you cannot accomplish are better not undertaken.

　　「至於親戚，你不應該當面讚美他們。如果他們有過失，你應該指出來，並且糾正他們的態度。如果他們值得，你應該用獎勵、讚美的方式來幫助他們。你尤其不應該寵溺兒孫、妻子和侍者。你應該用不太柔順又不太嚴厲的中庸方式使他們中規中矩。對於某些惡毒的人，最好嚴厲而非溫柔地加以訓誡。」

　　　鐃鈸和鼓被敲擊時，聲音是悅耳的。
　　　牆壁和帳篷的樁釘被擊打時，它們變得堅固。
　　　皮革和惡毒的人被打擊時，它們變得柔和。
　　　孩童被訓誡得宜時，他們變得順從。

"As for relatives, you shouldn't praise them to their faces. And if they have faults you should point them out and try to correct their attitudes. If they are worthy, try to help them with rewards and praises. In particular, you should not spoil children and grandchildren, wife, and servants. And you should keep them in line with moderate treatment, neither too soft nor too strict. In the case of certain vicious people, it is actually better to discipline them strictly rather than gently."

When cymbals and drums are beaten, the sound is sweet.

When walls and tent pegs are beaten they become sturdy.

When leather and vicious people are beaten they become tempered.

When children are properly disciplened, they become obedient.

「在某些情況下，有些愚蠢的人對自己擁有一個美好的家庭或朋友不知感恩，他們侮辱家人和朋友，與其爭鬥，使家人或朋友厭倦他們。但是與家人或朋友分離之後，卻感到懊悔。這是無法建立一段經久友誼的徵兆。」

獅子和狗過度交誼，獅子將受到狗的襲擊。
眼睛和眉毛的距離太近，眼睛將無法看見眉毛。

「沒有什麼比明瞭人的良莠品質更重要的了。我們不乏一個好人讓社群、村莊或國家安樂的例子，也不乏一個壞人在鄰居、社群和國家之間製造動亂的例子。」

"In certain cases some foolish people do not appreciate a good family or friend, and will insult them and fight with them, causing the family or friend to become tired of them. But after they are separated, they will feel regret. This is the sign of inability to establish a durable friendship."

If they associate too much, the lion will be insulted by dogs.

If they are too close, the eye cannot see the eyebrow.

"There is nothing more important than to know the good and bad qualities of people. There are cases in which a single good person makes a community, village, or country happy; and there are cases in which a single bad person creates trouble among neighbors, community, and countries."

結交傑出的朋友，你將變得傑出。

結交邪惡的朋友，你將變得邪惡。

一個善友比黃金更稀有難得。

如果這個善友跟你意見相左，與之結交。

一個邪惡的朋友比毒藥更糟糕。

即使這個邪惡的朋友站在你這邊，也最好拋棄。

「因此，明瞭朋友的良莠品質非常重要。」

If you associate with excellent friends you will become excellent.

If you associate with evil friends you will become evil.

A virtuous friend is rarer than gold.

If he is on another side, make a friend of him.

An evil friend is worse than posison.

Even if he is on your side, it is better to throw him away.

"So it is of primary importance to understand the good and bad qualities of your friends."

訓練自己的行止中庸

接著宗努洛登說：「請告訴我如何訓練自己的行止中庸。」

老人說：「啊，是的。行為是來、去、停留、工作、降伏敵人和服務親戚。舉止，舉例來說是飲食、睡覺、停留、說話和離開的禮節。你應該自我檢視並且詢問他人關於自己行為舉止的好與壞，擷取過去的範例，規劃未來，依照自己的能力來行動，並且遵守國家的體制。不要害怕有權有勢的人，也不要侮辱弱者。取決得失，以及什麼能做、什麼不能做。如果它是可以做的，應該不管其結果是大或小，你應該從一開始就小心謹慎，努力念頌祈願文來祈請成功和累積功德。」

一場演說的開場白是困難的，
一件工作的主要部分是困難的，
佛法的結行是困難的。

Then Zhonnu Loden said, "Please tell me how I should train myself in the action and conduct of moderation."

The old man said, "Oh ya ! The action is coming, going, staying, working, subduing enemies, and serving relatives. The conduct is, for example, the manner of eating, drinking, sleeping, staying, speaking, and going, In both action and conduct you should examine yourself what is good and bad and ask others, take examples from the past, plan for the future, act according to your own ability, and abide by the system of the country. Do not fear powerful people or insult weak people. Determine the gain and loss, what can be done and what cannot; and if it is done, whether the result will be large or small. You should be careful from the beginning and try to say prayers for the success of undertaking and accumulation of merits."

In a speech the beginning is difficult,

In work the main part is difficult,

In Dharma the conclusion is difficult.

　　「因此，不論你從事什麼樣的工作，都應該懷著勇氣和耐心來從事，直到完成。你的心不應該追逐眾人之口，應該善巧地堅持很長一段時間。最後，如果這件工作是好的，那麼你應該感到滿足。如果失敗了，你應該毫無悔恨地忍受，不責怪他人。只有兩個方法可以讓計畫成功：藉由智慧或藉由福德[17]的力量。透過三寶來積聚福德，乃是人們獲得今生與來世安樂的唯一方式。」

　　積聚少量的福德，

　　勝過動用九牛二虎之力。

17　功德〈福德〉（Merit）：善業，由身、語、意的善行所產生的能量。
　　為方便區分，本書譯者將菩薩的事業譯為功德，而一般人的善業譯
　　為福德。

"So whatever task you have undertaken, until it is completed you should work with courage and patience. Your mind should not run after the many mouths of many people, and you should persevere for a long time with skill. In the end, if the work is good, then you should be satisfied. If you failed, you should bear it without regret and without blaming others. There are only two ways for projects to succeed: by knowledge or by the strengh of merit. The only means for one's own happiness in this life and the next is to accumulate merit through the Three Jewels."

It is better to accumulate a spark of merit

Than to make efforts the size of a mountain.

又說：

藉由福德的力量所實現的目標
將如陽光般不倚賴任何事物。
藉由努力所實現的目標，
將如油燈的光亮般要仰賴眾多事物。

「不富裕的人不應該雄心勃勃地想要吃美饌、穿華服。他們不應該沈溺於粗魯愚蠢的活動，例如抽菸、飲酒和賭博。你應該日日夜夜非常小心、嚴謹地掙取和保護你的財富，不應該讓財富毫無用處地喪失或浪費。你不應該把財富借給不可靠的人，也不應該囤積窮人的物品來販賣。如果你藉由偷竊或狡猾的方式尋求財富，或因為忌妒而尋求財富，那麼你不但會失去財富，也會失去自己的性命。如果你以前沒有積聚善業，你無法僅僅透過努力就致富。」

And:

The purposes that are fulfilled by the strengh of merit
Will not depend on anything, like the light of the sun.
The purposes that are fulfilled by the strength of efforts
Will depend on many things, like the light of a butter lamp.

"People who are not wealthy should not be ambitious to eat fine food and put on fancy clothes. They should not indulge in crude and brainless activities like smoking, drinking, and gambling. You should earn and protect your own wealth day and night very strictly and carefully, and should not let it be lost uselessly or wasted. You should not lend to unreliable people, nor store with poor people's things that are to be sold. If you seek wealth by theft or cunning, or because of jealousy, you will end up by losing not only wealth but your own life. If you have no previously accumulated good karma, you will not prosper merely by efforts."

財富無法透過儲蓄取得，
要透過累積功德來取得。
衣物不會因為穿著而破損，
會因為福氣耗盡而消磨殆盡。
人們不會因為疾病而死亡，
是因為大限到來而離開。

「對富人而言，儘可能地把財富用於佛法是最好的方式。次好的做法是把財富用於利益他人。最末的做法是把財富用在自己的衣食上面。否則，當人們赤身空手地走向死亡時，就已經太晚了。」

如果你的心被黑暗覆蓋，
那麼即使如須彌山那樣的財富也幫不了你。

Wealth cannot be acquired by mere accumulation, but by accumulation of merit.

Clothes will not wear out by being put on, but because luck is exhausted.

People do not die from illness, they die when the time comes.

"It is best for rich people to spend their wealth for holy Dharma as much as they can. The next best thing is to use it for the benefits of others. The least good is to use it for their own back and mouth. Otherwise, when one leaves and one's property to go naked and empty-handed to death, it is too late."

If your mind is covered by darkness,
Even a heap of wealth like Mount Meru will not help you.

「一般而言,即使你的心是柔和的,也不應該失去自持。每當善緣或逆緣生起時,切勿太過急切地表達快樂或悲傷。你應該分辨誰善待你,誰惡待你。重複你所聽聞的每一件事情是錯誤的。」

說你心裡想到的每一件事是瘋狂的。

吃你所看到的每一樣東西是猶如豬狗的。

做你想到的每一件工作是沒大腦的。

"Generally, even if your mind is gentle, you should not lose your self-reliance. Do not be too hasty to express happiness or sorrow whenever good or bad arises. But you should distinguish between who does you good and who does you ill. It is wrong to repeat everything you have heard."

To say whatever comes into your mind is crazy.

To eat whatever you see is to be a dog or a pig.

To do whatever work you think of is brainless.

　　「在面對河川、斷崖峭壁、盜賊或野獸時，不要太過大膽。即使是輕微的危險，也要小心謹慎。即便是微小的協助，也要心懷感恩地接受。不論對方是好人還是壞人，都不要在他面前說其他人的壞話。少多嘴，心胸要更開闊。除了特殊而重要的情況或別無選擇的時候，不要說謊，要誠實。不要許下太多的承諾，要言出必行，如此才不會變成謊言。即使要付出你自身的財富或勞力，也要為了好人而英勇。勸導惡毒的人，不要讓他們變得頑固難馴。敬重並以食物接待陌生人，但不要把你的財產用在他們身上，也不要對他們顯露你的天性或訴說你的祕密。竭盡所能地幫助與你親近的人，但不要讓他們嫌惡你或對他們說謊。

"Don't be too bold facing rivers, precipices, thieves, or wild beasts. Be careful even the danger is small. Accept even minor assistance graciously. Do not say bad things about others in secret to anyone, good or bad. Be less talkative and more broad-minded. Except in special and important cases or when there is no choice, don't tell lies but speak honestly. Don't make many promises, but do whatever you have said so that it doesn't become a lie. Be brave for the sake of good people even if it costs your own wealth or labor. Reason with vicious people, and don't let them become obstinate. Receive strangers with respect and food, but don't lose property to them, and don't reveal your nature to them or tell your secrets. Do whatever you can to help people who are close to you, but don't make them disgusted with you or lie to them.

　　他人的地位貶低時，不要辱罵、虐待他們。當你顯耀、衣食豐足時，切勿自私自利，驕傲自大。不要試著挑戰喇嘛、首長、密續瑜伽士或苯教的權威。不要追隨善變、輕易感到快樂和悲傷的人。不要將他人所說的一切信以為真。不要把傷害你的人視為敵人，甚至不要對與你關係良好的人訴說祕密。即使你和某人爭吵，也不要挖掘對方隱密的過失。不要對已經逝去的人有所期待。不要對曾經幫助過你的人只有短暫的忠誠。不要倚賴你不太了解的人。在眾人之間不要多言。獨處時不要太過忙碌。任何時候都不要承擔太多的計畫。不要欺騙信任你的朋友。不要渴望他人的財富。不論你的工作是什麼，要合宜地從事，並且檢視它的目的。你要善解朋友的感受，你應該能夠直覺到他人的心。善用你的地位。即使你不貪婪，也要非常節省。你應該溫柔而堅定，誠實而謙遜。」

When the position of others has diminished, do not abuse them. When you are flourishing and full-belled, do not be selfish and proud. Don't try to challenge the solemn authority of lamas, chiefs, or tantric yogis and Bonpos. Don't follow the man who is fickle and who is quick to feel happiness and sadness. Don't take everything that other people tell you as true. Don't consider whoever harms you as an enemy. Don't tell secret even to people with whom you are on good terms. Even if you quarrel with someone, don't dig out his secret faults. Have no expectations of people who have gone away. Do not have short loyalty to a person who has been helpful to you. Do not rely on a person who you don't know well. Don't speak too much among many people. Don't be too busy when you are alone. Don't at any time undertake too many projects. Don't cheat the friends who believe in you. Don't hanker after the wealth of others. Whatever your work, do it in proportion to the job, and examine its purpose. Be sensitive to the feelings of your friends; you should be able to intuit other people's minds. Make use of your position. Even if you have no avarice, be very economical. You should be gentle but firm; honest and moderate."

「一般來說，你應該小心檢視他人的良莠品質。但是這年頭，大多數人都不會探究某人的行為是否有節有守。如果人們受到一點點的協助、恩惠或被投以微笑，他們很快地就給予讚美。如果願望受到阻撓，人們做了他們不喜歡的事情，就開始辱罵。間接傳來的讚美或誹謗，連聽都不要聽。」

學者自己知道如何分辨，

愚蠢的人跟隨他人所說的話。

一隻老狗發出聲響時，

其他的狗會無緣無故地奔跑。

"In general you should examine carefully the good and bad qualities of people. But nowadays most people do not inquire whether someone acts according to the ethics of a cultivated person. And if they receive a little help or benefit or are given a smile, they are quick to praise; but if their wishes are interfered with and something is done that they don't like, the abuse starts. Don't even listen to praise or disparagement that comes secondhand."

Scholars know how to discriminate by themselves,
Foolish people will follow what others say.
When an old dog makes noise,
for no reason other dogs will run.

又說：

話會隨著嘴巴愈傳愈多，
食物會隨著手愈傳愈少。

又說：

獨立自主是快樂的事情；
倚賴他人帶來悲傷。
共有的財產是爭吵的根源。
承諾是違背誓言的起因。
滿足於你所擁有的事物是最佳的財富。
利益他人的精神是最佳的特質。
知識是最佳的裝飾。
不存狡智的朋友是最佳的朋友。
生起菩提心是最佳的快樂。

And:

If talk goes from mouth to mouth it will increase,

If food goes from hand to hand it will decrease.

And:

Any independence is a happy thing;

All dependence on others involves sorrow.

Common property is the root of quarrels.

Promises are the cause of broken promises.

The best wealth is contentment with what you have.

The best quality is the spirit of benefiting others.

The best ornament is knowledge.

The best friend is the one without guile.

The best happiness is developing the Bodhi mind.

又說：

即便在愚人之中，也會有有錢人；
在野獸之中，也有些是英勇的。
動物也知道如何滿足牠們的願望。
但是在這個世界上，
博學多聞、舉止溫柔者少之又少。

因此，請修持溫柔者的道德倫常。

接著宗努洛登說：「喔，我非常感謝你給予這些詳細的教導。但是我很難記住這麼多，因此請精簡告知。」

And:

Even among fools there will be wealthy ones;

Among wild beasts some will be heroic.

Animals, too, know how to satisfy their wishes.

But the learned and gentle-mannered are rare in the world.

So please practice the ethic of gentle people.

Then Zhonnu Loden said, "Oh, I'm most thankful that you gave me these detailed instructions. But it is difficult to keep in mind so many instructions like these. So please tell them to me in a condensed form."

世俗倫常的五個重點

老人說：「喔，是的，你是對的。聽清楚我要說的話。世俗倫常可以歸納總結為五個重點：

一，溫柔的本性。

二，行止中庸穩健。

三，開闊的心胸和穩定的天性。

四，精於事先估計工作。

五，用誠實、利益他人的精神來從事一切活動。

「第一，如果你是一個憤怒、出言不遜的人，你將無法與任何人和諧共處。即使你幫助人，人們也不想接近你。最後，沒有人會見你或與你結交。因此，擁有溫柔的本性是必要的。溫柔的本性是指本性柔軟而放鬆，不對任何人發怒或口出惡言。但這不表示你應該像麝香鹿的皮革一般，可以被拉往任何方向；或像蜂蜜一般，黏著任何接觸到它的事物。」

The old man said, "Oh, ya, your're right. Listen and I will tell you. Now, if worldly ethics are summarized, they can be included in five points:

1. A gentle nature

2. Moderation in action and conduct

3. A broad mind and stable nature

4. To be good at estimating work in advance

5. In all activities to have an honest and beneficial spirit

"1. If you are a man of angry and harsh words, you will not be in harmony with anyone. Even if you help people, they won't want to come near you. In the end no one will see you or keep you company. So it is necessary to have gentle nature. A gentle nature means one whose nature is soft and relaxed, without angry or harsh words for anybody. But that doesn't mean that you should be like the leather of the musk deer, which goes in any direction that it is pulled; or like honey, which will stick to whatever touches it."

　　「第二，毫無節制地從事大量的工作是冒險的。有時候，這麼做的結果有益處，但是有時候，它會是一種損失，並成為他人的笑柄。因此在交誼或從事活動的時候，你應該行止中庸獨立，不要太常改變心意。工作節制有度，表示不論你從事什麼工作，都應該知道如何根據自己和其他參與者的本性與能力來節制工作。但這不表示你要做一個大膽愚蠢而不參與任何活動的人。」

"2. To do a lot of work without moderation is risky. Sometimes the result will be profitable, but sometimes it will be a loss and nothing but an object of ridicule. So in friendships or activities you should act moderately and independently without many changes of mind. Moderation in work means that whatever work you do, you should know how to moderate it according to your own nature and ability and those of the other people involved. But it does not mean to be a bold, foolish man who will not be involved in any work."

「第三，沒有人不想要食物、財富、女人等等。但是為了享受這些事物，你應該要考慮舉止謙遜、謹慎的後果和需要。沒有人不會對嚴苛的話語和造成傷害的行為發怒。但是你應該考慮到法律及其懲處，尤其是今生來世的因果業報法則。一個穩定的人，本性不會因為好或壞、快樂或悲傷而改變，到最後一定會受到大家的讚揚。因此，你應該要穩定，不要朝三暮四。穩定意味著不追逐你的念頭或任何人所說的話，你從事的活動和舉止是穩定不變的。這不表示你的背脊上有一條棍子而無法彎腰。」

"3. There is no one who does not desire food, wealth, women, and so forth. But in order to enjoy them you should consider the consequences and the need for being modest in behavior. There is no one who will not be angry at harsh words and harm done. But you should concern generally about the law and its punishments, and especially about the cause and result of karma in this life and the next. A stable person whose nature will not change in the midst of good or bad, happiness or sorrow, will certainly be praised by everyone in the end. So you should be stable without shifting in every direction. Stability means not running after whatever you think of or whatever anyone says, and that your activities and behaviors are constant. It does not mean having a stick down your backebone so that you cannot bend."

「第四，在從事所有活動的時候，你應該思量過去和未來。你應該檢視所有的得失利弊：什麼活動會對自己和他人帶來當前和未來的利益與傷害。如果知道如何檢視事物，你將合宜地達成心想之事。沒有時間加以檢視就去做某件事情，會影響所有人，不只影響像我們自己這樣的人，也會影響君主。舉例來說，帕威欽王（King Pa-we-Chin）和蘭卡王（King of Lanka）看到菩薩美拓達澤（Metog Dadzey）、仙人左帕瑪瓦（Rishi Zopar Mawa）和他們的王后在一起。

"4. In all activities you should give consideration to the past and future, And you should examine all the gain and loss, good and bad, what will be beneficial and what will be harmful to yourself and to others now and in the future. If you know how to examine things, you will achieve properly whatever you have in mind. Doing something without having time to examine it affects everyone, not only people like ourselves, but even kings. For example, King Pa-we-Chin [dPa'-Ba'i Byin] and the King of Lanka saw the Bodhisattva Metog Dadzey [Me-Tog Zla-mDzes] and the Rishi Zopar Mawa [Drang-Srong bZod-Par sMra- Ba] in the company of their queens.

　　於是他們想像美拓達澤和左帕瑪瓦想要透過貪欲來掌控他們的王后。這兩位國王把美拓達澤和左帕瑪瓦交給劊子手行刑。後來感到懊悔，卻無法補償他們的行為。人們聽從他人的話，狡猾行騙的故事也比比皆是。舉例來說，貝瑪札拉殺死了一個名叫桑嫫的女人，並且把沾滿血跡的刀子扔在一個名叫喬達摩的聖者前面，喬達摩因而受到懲罰。一個竊賊偷了一頭犢牛，把牛留在一個住在森林中的辟支佛[18]前面，然後就跑掉了，辟支佛因而受到懲罰。因此，不論做什麼工作，都要小心謹慎。」

18　辟支佛：沒有上師協助而自行修持證悟的人，這類證悟者不對他人傳授法教。

They imagined that the Bodhisattva and the Rishi wanted to keep the queens in their power through desire. The kings handed them over to executioners who killed them. Later the kings repented, but there was no way of atoning for their deeds. There are also stories of people who listened to others and cheated with cunning. For example, the cunning Peme Tsalag [Padma'i rTsa Lag] killed a woman named Zangmo [bZang-Mo] and threw the blood-stained knife in front of a sage named Gautama. And Gautama received the pusnishment. A thief stole a calf and left it in front of a Pratyekabuddha who was living in a forest, then ran away. The Pratyekabuddha received the punishment. So, whatever work you do, you should be careful."

在確定你了解之前，不要談論。

在確定誓約的意義之前，不要宣誓。

「檢視意味著去明瞭你所展開的工作是否會完成；如果會完成，它的結果會是什麼。如果你射出一枝箭，那箭不應該落在地面上。不論你從事什麼工作，那工作都不應該瓦解。但檢視不代表你可以指出並聰明地分析他人的過失，卻沒有一面察看自己過失的鏡子。」

Don't talk until you are certain that you understand.

Don't take oaths until you are certain of their meanings.

"To examine means to know whether whatever work one starts will be completed or not; and if completed, what the outcome will be. If you shoot an arrow, should not fall on the ground. Whatever work you do should not collapse. But to examine does not mean to lack a mirror in which to see your own faults, while pointing out other people's faults and analyzing them cleverly."

「第五，如果你擁有誠實利他的心，那麼不論你為自己
或他人從事什麼樣的工作，每個人的願望都會達成。在今
生，護法[19]會保護你，使你具有名望。每個人都將愛你、敬重
你，你將在來世自動成就佛法。不要讓自己與這種良善的發
心分離，是非常重要的。如果你對他人充滿敵意，自己將面
對嚴苛的後果。利益之念代表對所有人伸出援手的善念，不
論對方的地位高低、好壞，不考慮對方是否曾經幫助過自
己，或是否相識。它不只是對你自己的朋友、親戚、兒孫和
妻子充滿愛與感情。如果擁有這五種品質，即使沒有其他事
物，你也會是人上之人。」

19　護法：護法就是護持佛法，凡佛法所在之處，就有護法。護法一般
　　稱為金剛或明王。

"5. If you have an honest and altruistic mind, in whatever work you do for yourself or others, everybody's wishes will be achieved. In this life the Dharma Protectors will protect you and will make your name and fame flourish. Everyone will love and respect you, and you will automatically accomplish the Dharma for the next life. It is very important not to dissociate yourself from this good intention. If you have malice toward others, the consequences for yourself will be harsh. Beneficial thought means the good thought of giving help to all, high or low, good or bad, without considering whether they have helped you or are known to you. It is not just having love and affection for your own friends, relations, sons, grandsons, and wife. If you possess these five qualities, even if you possess no others, you shall be the most excellent of men."

不受染污的自私發心所控制

宗努洛登說：「即使人們知道這所有的教導，也很難付諸實修。這年頭，如果你注意大多數人說話的方式，似乎沒有人不是舉止溫柔、博學多聞。但若是觀察他們的所作所為，卻像是舉止粗魯的人。請告訴我，這是什麼緣故？」

老人說：「喔，宗努洛登，你要仔細聽好，並且謹記在心。這年頭的人明白這些道理卻無法實修，是因為他們被自私自利的發心和情緒所控制。」

　　愚蠢的人觀察時，
　　他們是聰明的，
　　一旦付託到他們手中的時候，
　　他們就一無所知。

Zhonnu Loden said, "Even if one knows all these instructions, it will be difficult to apply them in practice. Nowadays, if you notice how most people talk, it seems that there is no one who is not gentle mannered and learned. But if you watch what they're doing, it looks as though they are only people of crude behaviors. So please tell me, what is the reason for this state of affairs ?"

The old man said, "Oh, Zhonnu Loden, listen well and keep it in mind. The reason why people these days know but cannot practice is that they are overpowered by selfish motives and emotions."

Fools are clever when they watch,

But they don't know anything when it is entrusted to their hands.

　　「因此，讓染污掌控我們的心是錯誤的。如果人們受到貪愛的掌控，他將侵占公款，誘拐女人，訴訟纏身。他將摧毀法器，欺騙朋友，殺害他人。如果他受到瞋怒的掌控，他將毆打、辱罵父母，心懷怨恨，訴說朋友的過失。他將因毆打、殺害、與人爭執，為自己和他人帶來悲傷。如果受到驕慢的控制，他的心將充滿自我和自滿，輕視嘲笑他人，數落他人的過錯，仇視下屬。如果他受到嫉妒的控制，他將毀謗、中傷上位者和對手，嫉妒同等地位的人，並且因為他人擁有地位、權勢和財富而不快樂。

"So it is wrong to allow one's mind to be overpowered by defilements. If a person is overpowered by passion, he will steal the wealth of others of embezzle funds, snatch women, and get into lawsuits. He will destroy sacred objects, cheat friends, and take the lives of others. If he is overpowered by anger, he will beat and abuse his parents, harbor resentments, and tell the faults of friends. He will afflict himself and others with sorrow by beating, killing, and quarreling with everybody. If he is overpowered by pride, his mind will sweel up with egoism and conceit, he will be contemptuous and mocking, repeat the faults of others, and feel hatred for inferiors. If he is overpowered by jealousy, he will slander and speak ill of superiors, rival and be envious of equals, and be unhappy because of the power, wealth, and position of others.

　　如果他受到貪婪的控制，他將無法佈施財富來行供養或
幫助他人，也無法協助或借貸給他人。他永遠不會感到滿
足，甚至無法把財富用在自己的衣食上面，他是真正的餓
鬼。如果他受到無明[20]的控制，他將完全不知道如何積聚善德
或清淨惡業、什麼樣的工作是好的或壞的、誰是好人或壞
人，以及該接受什麼、該排拒什麼。他將留在迷妄之中。如
此一來，六垢[21]、五毒[22]加上貪婪，將為他帶來今生和來世的
所有痛苦。由於他不是自持的，因此將受控於充滿染污的自
私發心——根據修行倫常和世俗倫常，這種發心是一切錯誤
行為的根源。

20　無明（Ignorance）：看待眾生和事物的錯誤方法，認為眾生和事物
　　是真實存在的、獨立自主的、堅實的、及與生俱來的。
21　六垢：
（1）以驕慢心聞法，認為自己足可媲美上師。
（2）缺乏信心聞法，專挑上師與法教的毛病。
（3）冷漠對待法教，認為有無受法皆無關宏旨。
（4）不是被周遭事物分心〔掉舉〕，就是內弛而昏昏欲睡〔昏沉〕。
（5）煩躁，認為講法太冗長或外境無趣。
（6）氣餒，認為沒有能力修法或證悟成佛。
22　五毒：貪、嗔、痴、慢、嫉。

If he is overpowered by avarice, he will not be able to part with wealth to make offerings or give help. He will not be able to give assistance or loans to others. The time will never come when he fells he has enough. He will not be able even to use his wealth for his own clothing or food. He is the real hungry ghost. If he is overpowered by ingorance, he will not know anything about how to accumulate virtues or purify evil deeds, what kind of work is good or bad, who is a good man or a bad man, and what to accept and what to reject; he will remain in confusion. In this way, the six defilements, the five poisons plus avarice, will bring him all the undesirable sufferings of this life and the next. Since he is not self-reliant, the defiled selfish motives, which are the root of all wrong actions according to both spiritual and worldly ethics, are free to have their way with him.

因此，如果你想要在今生來世享受安樂，就不要一直談
論他人的品質，而要觀察自己，檢視自己的心。糾正自己的
本性，留在正道之上。這是達成修行和世俗成就的方法。
喔，聰穎的孩子，你明白嗎？你再仔細聽：

財富是大得和大失的起因；
藉由供養和佈施來滋長福德、
乃財富具有意義的目的。
難得的人身只有這麼一次；
持守布薩[23] 和居士的戒律。
瞋怒是投生地獄之因。
披上忍辱的盔甲。

---

23 布薩〈齋戒、靜齋〉（Upavasatha）：廣義言之，指清淨身心，而慎
     防身心之懈怠；狹義而言，則指八關齋戒，或特指過午不食之戒
     法。齋之梵語音譯烏逋沙他、布薩陀婆，略譯為布薩。蓋凡有持
     齋，則必有戒，故齋戒二字自古並稱。

Now, if you desire to enjoy happiness in this life and the next, don't keep talking about other's qualities, but watch yourself and examine your own mind. Correct your own nature and keep yourself on the right path. This is the entire means of achieving both spiritual and worldly accomplishments. Oh, intelligent son. did you understand ? Listen to them again:

Wealth is the cause of great gain and loss;

Generate merits by offering and giving, the meaningful purpose of wealth.

The human body, difficult to obtain, is only for this one time;

Keep the precepts of upavasatha and upasaka.

Anger is the cause of taking rebirth in hell,

Put on the armor of patience.

怠惰將無法達成今生或來世的目標。

要如同河水的流動般精進。

心思散漫的人浪費他們的人生。

把自己完全投入於充滿意義的善德。

為了明瞭如何應用這兩種道德倫常，

要修持聞、思、修。

驕慢的人永不饜足。

嫉妒的人永不快樂。

充滿貪欲的人永不滿足。

瞋怒的人永不和諧。

吝嗇的人永不感到充足。

愚癡無明的人永不成功。

Laziness will not achieve the aim of this life or the next.

Be diligent like the current of a river.

Distracted people waste their human life.

Devote yourself totally to meaningful virtues.

In order to know how to apply the two ethics,

Parctice hearing, pondering, and meditation.

Arrogant people will never be satisfied.

Jealous people will never be happy.

Lustful people will never be content.

Angry people will never be harmonious.

Stingy people will never be replete.

Ignorant people will never succeed.

迷妄的心永不自在。
少一點染污的情緒，就少一點痛苦。
當染污的情緒止息，痛苦也將止息。
因此，如果能夠遠離情緒染污的這個敵人，
那就太棒了。
情緒染污是一切痛苦之源。」

　　老人慢慢地起身。宗努洛登充滿真誠的喜悅、快樂和信任。他一邊向老人頂禮，一邊說：

喔，光輝時期的人如同格言的寶礦。
慈祥的父母和長輩是溫柔者的核心。
這樣的教導如同心要，
我以前從未聽聞。

Deluded minds will never be at ease.

If there is less defiled emotion, there is less suffering.

When the defiled emotions have ceased, suffering will cease.

So it is excellent if you can do away with the

enemy, emotional defilements,

Which are the source of all undesirable happenings."

Slowly the old man stood up. Zhonnu Loden was filled with heartfelt, happiness, and trust; and he said, prostrating himself and showing respect to the old man:

O !The man of the glorious period of time

Is like a mine of the Jewel of Sayings !

The gracious parents and the older generation

Are the heart of the gentle people.

Such an instruction like the heart's quintessence

I have never heard before.

今日藉由博學老者的恩惠，
一個孤兒得到了父母的忠告。
未來請如父親對兒子一般，
一再給予教導。
殊勝者，你的恩惠無以為報，
願我能夠一再地見到你安樂的面容！

　　老人感到欣慰，他面容仁慈地說：「喔，是的，是的，親愛的孩子！好好保重，好嗎？」然後慢慢地走開。

Today by the grace of the learned old man

Advice has come to an orphan from his parents;

In the future, like a father to his son,

Please give instructions again and again.

Precious one, your graciouness is unrepayable,

May I see your happy face again and again !

The old man was amused, and with a kindly look he said, "Oh, ya, ya, dear boy ! Stay well, all right ?" and slowly he went on his way.

國家圖書館出版品預行編目資料

遇見‧巴楚仁波切 / 巴楚（Patrul）作 ; 項慧齡
　譯 .-- 初版 . -- 高雄市：雪謙文化出版：
　全佛文化發行 , 2008.9
　　面 ；　公分 , --（精選大師系列；1）
　譯自：The heart-essencc advicc on two
ethics
ISBN 978-986-81149-4-4（平裝）

1.　藏傳佛教 2.　佛教修持 3.　倫理學
226.965　　　　　　　　　　97017025

精選大師系列 01

遇見・巴楚仁波切

作　　　者：巴楚仁波切（Patrul Rinpoche）

顧　　　問：堪布烏金・徹林（Khenpo Ugyen Tsering）

譯　　　者：項慧齡

審　　　定：劉婉俐

編　　　輯：吳若寧

企　　　劃：劉小慧

封 面 設 計：陳光震

發 行 人：張滇恩　葉勇瀅

出　　　版：雪謙文化出版社

戶　　　名：雪謙文化出版社

銀 行 帳 號：兆豐國際商業銀行 三民分行（代碼 017）
　　　　　　040-090-20458

劃 撥 帳 號：42305969

手機：0963-625129　傳真：02-2917-6058

http:// www.shechen.org.tw　e–mail ：shechen.book@gmail.com

台灣雪謙佛學中心

高 雄 中 心：高雄三民區中華二路 363 號 9F-3
　　　　　　電話：07-313-2823 傳真：07-313-2830

台 北 中 心：台北市龍江路 352 號 4 樓
　　　　　　電話：02-2516-0882 傳真：02-2516-0892

行 銷 代 理：紅螞蟻圖書有限公司

地　　　址：台北市內湖區舊宗路 2 段 121 巷 28、32 號 4 樓

電　　　話：02–2795-3656　傳真：02–2795-4100

出 版 日 期：西元 2008 年 9 月初版
　　　　　　西元 2014 年 2 月初版二刷

ISBN 978-986-81149-4-4（平裝）

定　　　價：新臺幣 200 元